Tribulations
of
A Wandering Soul

by
Cory Fluharty

Edited by
Hodge Podge

Artists
Dave Saunders, Heather Reynolds, Bethany Tussing

© 2007 by Cory Fluharty.

To obtain permission or to contact the author, go to the website: www.silverbeargraphics.com and email us via the contact page. For additional information you may also send a request in writing to Cory Fluharty's publisher:
SilverBear Graphics
9 Westminster S/C, #333
Westminster, MD 21157

You may order additional copies of this book by emailing the publisher at: info@silverbeargraphics.com, or by logging onto www.silverbeargraphics.com and using the "Buy It Now" button under the *Buy A Book* page on the website.

Fluharty, Cory *Tribulations of A Wandering Soul*
ISBN 9780977807000

First Edition: June 2006
Second Edition: April 2007

And so
it begins...

PROLOGUE

While wondering through the mountains of Colorado I came across one of the strangest individuals I'd ever met. He had long nappy hair and a beard that hung past his shoulders. His wardrobe consisted of a long gray jacket with holes, a pair of torn up camouflage jeans, and for the life of me, I still don't know what the hell he was wearing on his feet. They kind of looked like camel toes. Anyway, whatever, I found this weird character meditating underneath a tree by the river.

At first I really didn't know what to say. I didn't want to bother him. He looked so peaceful. He opened his eyes looked at me, smiled, and said, "Hello my friend, isn't it a beautiful evening?"

"Yes it is." I answered, kind of bewildered, wondering why he had a smirk on his face. It was almost as if he knew something I didn't.

So I asked him, "When you sit and meditate, what do you think about?"

He grinned and said, "I was listening to the river. It was telling me its secrets about life." I gave him a weird look and wondered what the hell he was on.

He asked me if I had any smoke and I replied, "Yes but you'll have to come back to my camp with me."

As we were walking he told me he had been in the mountains for days contemplating all the things that nature had taught him. I asked him if he would like to join my friends and me for dinner. He smiled and said, "I would love to hang with you and your friends. I'm David. And you are?"

"Oh, I'm sorry, my name is Logan, and it's nice to meet you."

As we all settled down by the fire after dinner I asked him, "So tell me man, what is your deal? I'm sure you've got a few stories you could tell. I'm not dissing you by any means, it's just it's not every day you run into someone sitting by a river meditating and talking about how the river is telling him secrets about life."

He looked at me and said, "It's not really a secret. Life is always telling you answers, it's just a question of whether or not you're listening."

"Alright, so let's hear it man, curiosity is getting the best of me."

And, of course, with that damn smirk on his face, he looked up at me and said, "I'm going to have to roll one up and think about where to begin, there is so much to tell. Oh well, it's not like you're going to believe me anyway. No words could do justice to the things I've seen in life, but I'll do my best." Just like that, he spun one up, lit it on fire, and commenced to telling me his story:

~

"I have met so many beautiful characters in my life, like my friend Michael. The things this man could do with his hands were beyond me. He could spin a staff in one hand while holding a sphere in the other hand, rolling it around his body while they were both on fire. He had this excited look on his face, like you would see on a child. When you looked in his eyes, you could see nothing but compassion. I sat down next to him one day and said, "My friend, you are one of the most humble men I have ever met, and you can flow like water. Tell me, what is your secret?"

He smiled at me, handed me two spheres and said, "Rotate these in your hand until they no longer touch each other."

Now I tried it for hours, and I couldn't figure out how to spin two spheres around each other without touching. I went back to him and said, "I don't understand, maybe my hands are just too small."

He laughed. "It's not your hands. The trick is to relax and to 'play more, think less'."

I looked at him with a confused look on my face. He smiled and said, "Trust me my friend, you'll see."

So I sat, relaxed myself and started to rotate the spheres. "Now let go of trying to move the spheres and let them move you."

As I sat there, I realized that, the less I thought about it and the more relaxed I became, the easier it was to rotate the spheres in my hand until finally they no longer touched each other.

He smiled, "You see, I told you, 'think less, play more'. The moment you stop clouding your mind with assumptions on how to do it and just let your body feel the flow of the spheres, without expectations, you are then just being in the moment. Then you see that the spheres are not separate from you, but are a part of you, an extension of your body, if you will, much like most things in this world."

He smiled, looked over at all the different toys he had to play with and said, "You know, each one of those toys taught me a lot about life, the most important of which was that true power lies in patience and gentleness."

~

Then I guess I could tell you about Carlos. To this day, he is still one of the wisest men I have ever met. I will forever be in his debt for the things he has taught me. He was a true ladies' man who had spent many years in the Special Forces. He knew five different styles of martial arts, and had a look in his eyes of a man who had seen many battles in his time.

One day I went to him and said, "My friend we have known each other for years. Your skills have surpassed anyone I have ever met. Will you teach me Kung-Fu?"

Carlos looked at me, "Tell me, my friend, why should I teach you anything?"

"Well, to make a long story short, while I was in Hawaii I met a man who spent many days showing me the ways of his people. He told me that I would never truly understand myself until I learned to control my emotions. So I asked him how to do that. He said that my intuition would show me the way. So here I am my friend, talking to you because, for some reason, my gut is telling me that you can help me some how.

Without a word, Carlos walked away. I thought, "Great, there goes the whole listening to my gut theory. Oh well, I tried."

As I got up to leave, Carlos showed up with two Crystal sticks in his hands. "When you can wield these two sticks around your body without hitting yourself, then I will teach you Kung-Fu."

"What do you mean by wielding these sticks?"

He then picked up the two Crystal sticks and started moving his arms in circular motions. I stood there in total amazement as I watched him spin the sticks around his arms, and then around his neck.

I looked at him. "How did you do that? I mean, that was insane!"

He smiled and started laughing, *"Endurance, perseverance, and patience my friend. When you understand these things, you will come to find a deeper essence of learning how to use your mind to ponder as you train."*

I spent months spinning Crystal sticks, hitting myself in the face, trying to understand what he meant by pondering while I trained. Until one day, I finally understood what he meant. It no longer became a task, but a form of meditation.

Months passed until finally Carlos returned from his travels, *"So show me what you've learned."*

"Sure, let me get my sticks."

"No, that's not what I meant." Without warning, he started swinging his fists at me. To my surprise, without thought, I started blocking him. *"Good my friend, now you're ready to be taught."*

"I don't understand Carlos, what was that all about?"

"You see David, I gave you those Crystal sticks because they teach you fluid circular movements, and every time you do something a thousand times, it becomes imbedded in your muscle memory, thus giving you the ability to react without thought because your body already knows what needs to be done. That's why, now, when you spin the Crystal sticks, it has become such a meditation, because you have become detached from the situation, which gives you the ability to focus on calming the mind. The reason for this is that when the mind is tied up, it feels inhibited in every move it makes, and nothing will be accomplished with any sense of spontaneity." *"Why didn't you tell me all of this when you first gave me the Crystal sticks?"*

"Do you think that you would have understood? Some things you must first experience before you can truly understand. Besides, I needed to test your sincerity about wanting to learn Kung-Fu, and you definitely have a strong will my friend. Tomorrow we will begin your lessons."

"Thank you, Carlos, for being so patient with me. Sorry I questioned you."

"That's okay, David. You must first question in order to truly understand."

Many years have passed since I last saw Carlos, but I still find myself learning from the lessons he taught me. Sometimes, during training, I sit there, laugh to myself, and think, *"Oh, that's what you meant. Now I understand."*

~

Once, on a full moon, I was walking through the desert with my friends. We were going to have a drum jam and go on a vision quest. You could feel the potency of the energy in the air. You could tell that this was going to be one of those intense nights you never forget. I couldn't wait.

As the night passed by and the tea was being finished, my friend asked me if I would walk her home. She didn't know the way. As I left her at her tent, I gave her a kiss good night and started on my way back to the jam.

As I was walking, I remembered how long of a walk it was. Or was I lost? I figured I would listen for the drums to find my way back. I started walking and heard a faint beat so I kept going. I stopped to pull a piece of cactus off my jacket and realized that the beat I had been hearing was the jugs of water in my backpack beating against each other. I started laughing and thought, "I've been following the beat of my own drum. Oh well I guess my quest has started with a leap of faith in that my intuition will guide me there."

I continued my journey and, sure enough, I heard the drums in the distance. They were getting louder by the moment. As I got closer, the jam was picking up. I decided I should hurry and began to run as fast as I could go. I then felt this familiar feeling come over me and stopped dead in my tracks. There standing before me was my old friend Snake. I know you're thinking, "What the hell kind of name is Snake?" We call him that because that's his preferred style of Kung-fu other than dragon.

"Hello, my friend, I've been waiting for you." He smiled, lifted his hands in front of him, got into stance and said, "You know why I'm here."

"But of course, my friend. It would be an honor." I raised my hand to his and the sparring began. As we danced around each other, my visions became stronger and I noticed that Snake was no longer himself. What stood before me was me. As we flowed back and forth, I closed my eyes and saw that what I was facing was my own anxieties and fears. I embraced my fears of being hit, and of whether or not I was a good fighter, and of what his next move was. I let it all go. My thoughts clung to nothing, which in turn left them open to everything. I noticed everything began to slow down and I was no longer striving, I was just being in the moment.

I opened my eyes to see Snake smiling at me. "That's the fastest I've ever seen you. When you closed your eyes, what did you see?"

"I saw myself, my expectations, my fears and my desires. I let them go so I could embrace the moment for what it really was. I sought to be truly in the moment and as I entered that place, I felt everything slow down. Without thought, I was exactly where I needed to be. I realized that my enemy is simply a mirror of the dark places within my mind. I learned to be compassionate and to understand that it is nothing more than another perspective that will help me grasp the nature of the universe. It helped me to see that my enemy is really my brother showing me my weaknesses, to smile and embrace him with love."

Snake laughed, "I knew there was a reason you were one of my favorites to fight. I've been having visions too. Mine showed me some more dragon style."

"So what brought you out here anyway?" I asked.

"I was looking for someone to flow with and my gut told me I would find you by the drum jam next to the wash."

I walked over the hill and ran into my friend Jester. He said, "What's up my friend, how has your night been? Would you like to flow? I'd love to show you what I've learned tonight."

Without a word, we began to dance in the moonlight. Jester explained to me about how he had a vision. About how water flowed, how the tide pushed and pulled. He danced around me in beautiful fluid movements. He asked me of the lesson I learned. I told him, "I learned that my biggest enemy comes from within, and that through discipline and understanding of life I will learn how to overcome my issues and see them for what they truly are, emotional attachments. Is it me, Jester, or can you feel it too, like something is shifting consciously? The full moon, the energy in the air, the insane drum beats and all the visions we've had tonight, the synchronicity of it all, where do you begin to explain or understand?"

Jester just started laughing. "You know what your problem is, brother? You think too much. It is what it is and the answers will come when you need them. Leave it at that. Smile more, think less."

"That's why I love you, Jester. Leave it to you to make something so complex seem so simple. Maybe you're right."

~

One day while sitting at a lake in Texas, I saw one of the elders. His name was Abe. He had been traveling since I could remember. I had been troubled all day and thought maybe he could enlighten me on how to deal with it.

"So Abe, you've been around for a while, got any advice on how to deal with the stresses of life?"

He smiled, "Walk with me David; I want to show you something."

As we walked down a road of dirt and leaves, we came upon a patch of bamboo trees. "As you watch the bamboo blow to and fro, can you see the beauty it's trying to show? As they grow older, they learn to bend, to complement nature, not go against it. I wonder, if we could be as flexible as a bamboo tree, to complement nature with every bend, is that not the true way of a humbled man? Remember this one word- adaptability. When you understand this your troubles will be lightened." He then smiled with a twinkle in his eye and walked away. To this day every time I see a bamboo tree, I think about what he said.

~

This next story is about my friend Albright. To this day, I still have yet to meet a man who radiates as much love as him. One day while sitting at the top of a hill looking down on a quarry below, I was distraught because I spent an entire week trying to help a fellow traveler, who my friends had found homeless in Ohio sitting on a curb, starving and strung out from a drug binge. I did the best I could to help her kick her habit; I gave her a place to stay, food, clothes and got her a job. But I woke up one morning to find that she packed up and left with some random trucker passing by. I stood there going back and forth in my head: Had we mistreated her in some way? Did I not give her a home, food, clothes? I got her a job, what else could I have done? While I stood there, driving myself crazy with my thoughts, I felt a warm feeling of love come over me. Then I felt a hand on my shoulder and I heard a gentle voice behind me say, "Brother, stop stressing. You did your best."

"Albright, what are you doing here?"

"I came to comfort you, my friend."

"How did you know I was down here?"

"A little birdie told me. David, why are you letting this eat at you?"

"Because I thought I could make a difference, that maybe I could help her with her issues."

Albright smiled. "You did David. You showed her compassion. You gave her love and opportunity. It's not your fault that she didn't stay. Only she knows her path, my friend. Just because she's not where you want her to be, doesn't mean she isn't where she's supposed to be. You did your best, David, have faith. See, your problem lies in the fact that you gave her love with conditions."

"What do you mean, Albright? Explain."

"See, you gave her love with the hope that she would clean up her act. And when that expectation wasn't met, you felt disappointed. You see, brother, that is the problem with most people in this world. The giving and receiving of love is one of the most important lessons we are here to learn. When you can love freely and not expect anything in return, then you will finally understand the true meaning of love. If you cross paths with someone who doesn't want love, allow them space, for this is also love. And don't forget to love yourself my friend. When you learn this you will radiate love and you will never have to look far to find it. And when you walk with love, compassion and self understanding long enough, you will finally come to understand why the sages respect all life." Then he gave me a big hug.

"Thank you, Albright; you are such a beautiful person."

"So are you, David, don't ever forget that. Have faith that your heart will always lead you to where you need to be, my friend. And worry will never find you."

~

One of the greatest men I've ever met, I guess you could say he is the king of the gypsies. Whenever there is a problem, he's always one of the first people there to help resolve it. His name is Rook. One night I saw him sitting at the bar, so I walked over, sat down next to him and said, "You know, I just want to thank you for everything you've done for our community. So tell me, how do you do it? How do you keep the peace?"

"Well, David, let me see, I guess the best way to explain it would be... Okay, its like being in a bar, everyone is drunk except for you. You can see everyone else acting irrational and being emotional. But, because you're sober, you know that most of their issues are petty. It's kind of like that when you finally become an aware person. You see that most people see their world through their emotional wounds and are not aware of it. That most people just want to be loved and accepted as they are. If you give them that, they will feel no need to be hostile. Always be compassionate to your brothers and sisters, even if they don't deserve it. Remember, hatred condemns and love redeems."

I smiled. "You know, you truly are a sage. I don't know what we would do without you my friend. Thank you for the words of wisdom."

~

As the night went by David told me more about the tribe of gypsies that he had wandered around the country with for a while. He also told me about tour and how he had hung out with a group called the "Hippie Mafia". He told me about their downfall to greed and how he spent years secretly training in the martial arts with hippie ninjas in the woods. He also told me about a group of lost boys who taught him that the secrets of the universe are told by nature, that if you look close enough and quiet your mind, that nature is constantly trying to show you the way.

He looked me dead in the eyes and said, "Brother, I know these things seem hard to believe, but please lend me your ear. I promise you'll see that it's not the right answer that shows the wisdom you know, but being able to ask the right questions, that is the way to go. One must first discipline and control one's own mind to find the key to one's soul. Close your eyes, quiet your mind and learn to let it all go. Truth comes when your mind is purged of all things, when there is no sense of striving or care. It is when the mind is very quietly listening timelessly to everything that you become aware. Your gaze becomes fixed on what unites rather than divides you. Glimpse the unity behind the diversity. Shit, what was I saying? Damn I'm high."

I looked at him and said, "Man, after saying all that you're just going to end it with, "I forgot what I was saying?" What the hell is that?"

"Well, that's how it goes, right? When you think you know what the hell is going on, you realize you only see the tip of the iceberg. How magical and beautiful this place really is. Besides, I've come to the realization that you won't understand what I'm talking about until you experience it for yourself."

I looked at him and said, "On that note my friend, I'm going to bed. All these crazy ass stories have made the night fly by. I hope you are around tomorrow. Even if the stories you've told me aren't true, you've got one hell of an imagination my friend."

He looked at me, grinned and said, "So if you're ever in the desert and you come across a transvestite, a clown, a short man in a cloak and an old man with a long white beard, don't be afraid. They are all shamans."

At this point I thought, "This monucka is nuts. Oh well, I'll worry about it in the morning." I said my goodnights, laid down, looked over to the fire and watched him stare into the campfire with an intense look in his eyes just like when I first met him by the river. As I started to nod out and fall asleep, I remembered the last thing I heard come out of his mouth, "You may come to understand the rivers but are you bold enough to try and comprehend the depths of the sea?"

I woke up the next morning and the fire was out. I wondered if the night before had really happened or if that man was just a dream; but as I was cleaning my camp, I found a book titled: "Tribulations of a Wandering Soul." I opened it and in the left corner was written, "I looked inside and asked myself the questions that I had searched so long to find. What I found were the answers I was looking for, I just had to open my eyes and realize that the choice always was and always will be in my hands."

Later on that day as I was driving down the mountain I looked in my rearview mirror and swore I saw a small group of hippies wandering off into the mountains.

Many years have passed and I've grown to have my own children. I sit around and joke about the crazy ass hippie I met on the side of the mountain, and once in a great while I go up there, sit by the river and think about the things he wrote about. Is it really what I choose it to be? Am I really only limited by my own ignorance? I must first question in order to truly understand.

Sometimes I look up into those mountains and swear I see a glimpse of hippies in the mist. I hear something whisper to me, "You may come to understand the rivers, but are you bold enough to try and comprehend the depths of the sea?"

So that's my story. Sure, what I just told you sounds a little crazy. You know it's kind of funny, years ago, the hippie said the same thing to me. I guess he's right, you really can't understand until you experience it for yourself. So now, I leave you this book to prove to you that my story is true.

Yours truly,

Logan

DEDICATION

To my mother and father, Bonnie and Timmy; to my family: Charlotte, Dave, Douglas, Kristie, Susan, Drummer Steve, Eric, Adam, Heather, Justin, Kevin, Maggie, Dylene, Will, Renee, Bethany and Frank. To Heidi for giving me a passion for poetry. And to every person that I have ever met - you have all been my teacher in one form or another; for that, I am eternally grateful.

in Peace, Empathy, Compassion and Love,

PREFACE

For some reason or another, people have forgotten that they are gifted with free will, which means each individual has the right to perceive the world as they choose. You can see the world as heaven, or you can see it as hell, it is your choice.

You truly *are* the master of your own reality. Regrets are nothing more than not being able to understand something in your past. Let go of it, not everything is meant to be understood. Life is full of mystery; that's what makes it so beautiful. *You* are the author of your own story; so what will you choose it to be? It can either be a story of drama and turmoil, or a story of a person who uses the rocks that life throws as the stepping-stones to creating a beautiful world.

Ask yourself this question: "Do I like where I am standing, and if not, what can I do to change it? Or, is it really the place or the way I *perceive* things that I need to change?" You must first question in order to understand. You always have choices. Whether or not you *agree* with them is another story... but, you always have options. Remember that this book is nothing more than another perspective. Whether or not you see truth in it depends on how you perceive it, the choice is always yours. I can no more give you the answers or the truth you seek, than you can give me answers. However, I *can* give you my perspective, in hopes that together, we might find common ground.

DEFINITION OF THE WORD "HIPPIE"
FROM THE DICTIONARY:

Person who rejects established institutions and values and seeks spontaneity, direct personal relations expressing love, and expanded consciousness; often expressed externally in the wearing of casual, folksy clothing.

TABLE OF CONTENTS

REFLECTIONS

A man bound hand and foot by cause and effect
can not free another so they say
So I must learn to find a way
to unlock these shackles that hold me at bay
The answers I seek are not in a book
so I continue on my search
I continue to look
through all my adventures
and all my affairs
The answers I searched for
couldn't be found anywhere
So I closed my eyes
and became aware
So through these poems
I hope to share
The answers I found
within my lair

FIRST PATH: PHYSICAL

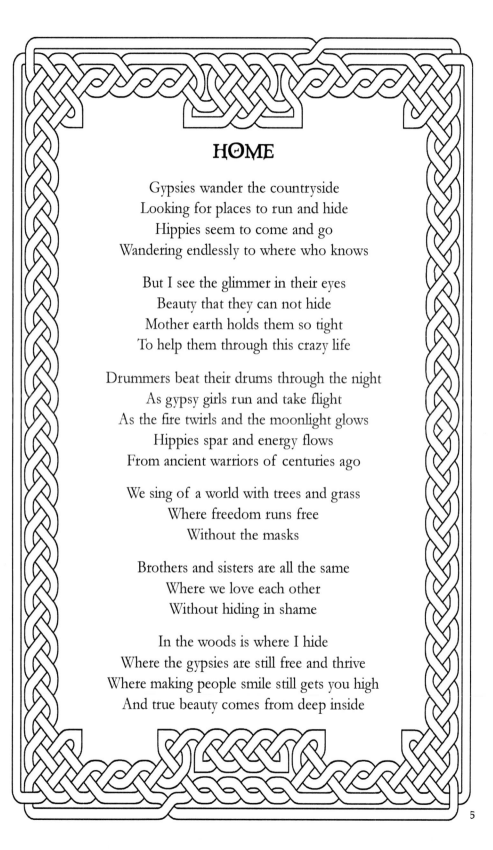

HOME

Gypsies wander the countryside
Looking for places to run and hide
Hippies seem to come and go
Wandering endlessly to where who knows

But I see the glimmer in their eyes
Beauty that they can not hide
Mother earth holds them so tight
To help them through this crazy life

Drummers beat their drums through the night
As gypsy girls run and take flight
As the fire twirls and the moonlight glows
Hippies spar and energy flows
From ancient warriors of centuries ago

We sing of a world with trees and grass
Where freedom runs free
Without the masks

Brothers and sisters are all the same
Where we love each other
Without hiding in shame

In the woods is where I hide
Where the gypsies are still free and thrive
Where making people smile still gets you high
And true beauty comes from deep inside

TRIBULATIONS OF THE NUGGET

These tribulations from within
Is where this story will begin
How many times have you walked this road?
Where your mind is clouded
And you don't know which way to go

Pop a squat
Smoke a bowl
And look at some grass
You know these moments of frustration will pass
There's no point in worry
It's not good for the soul
You're going to have to learn to let it all go

So hit the joint
Don't forget to pass
Remember these moments burn up
Like that joint you just passed
Make the most of these moments
Because they may be all that you have

These intricate moments are slowly displayed
As time passes by and the day fades away
There's laughter in the air and nuggs being fried
These beautiful moments are so hard to describe

Where smoking bowls with your friends
Is a daily affair
Waking every morning with birds chirping
And the smell of fresh air

There's nuggs being burned
And times flying by
I better hurry
I may lose my chance to get high

Oh like I was saying
These moments are so hard to describe
These intricate moments that fly by
So does any of this matter
When it's all said and done?
Fuck it, let's just burn another one

STRANGE DAYS

Once upon a time I sat on a mountain
And meditated for six hours to try to find
What was beyond all the
madness and baggage within my mind

As I sat and meditated I felt something
circle my head a few times
So I opened my eyes to see a humming bird
hovering around me the whole time

It was bright green with a violet neck
It stared at me for a moment, then kissed me
with its tongue right between my eyes

Then looked at me for a second and then it flew away
Then I felt this warm sensation of love and tranquility
come over me

Man what a day
Two days later while unloading a swing
I hear this cracking noise and
then a loud boom above me
Then I saw this bright white light
And felt this pain go through my whole body

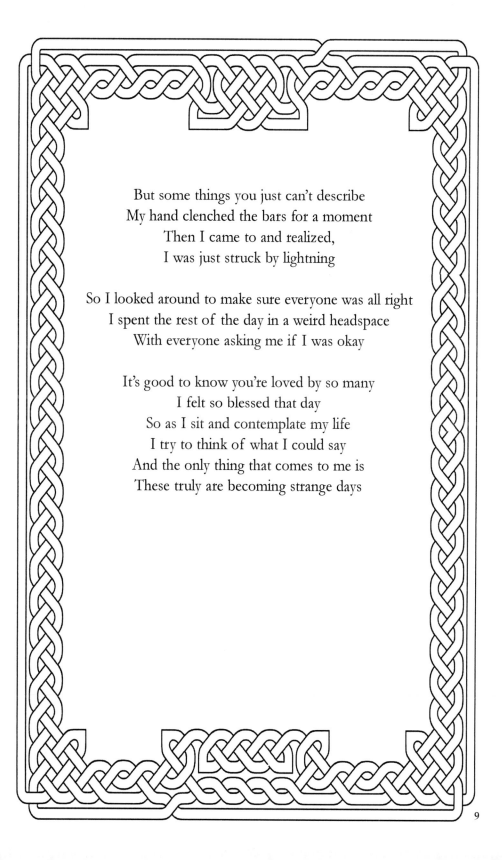

But some things you just can't describe
My hand clenched the bars for a moment
Then I came to and realized,
I was just struck by lightning

So I looked around to make sure everyone was all right
I spent the rest of the day in a weird headspace
With everyone asking me if I was okay

It's good to know you're loved by so many
I felt so blessed that day
So as I sit and contemplate my life
I try to think of what I could say
And the only thing that comes to me is
These truly are becoming strange days

DESERT

I do declare this place is nuts
With cactus and mountain, shrubs and dust
Now I remember why I love this place
The desert speaks to me in such subtle ways

Of things long forgotten, things in our past
Mama cries out,
"Please change your ways or this won't last"

But we forgot how to listen
So her screams are in vain
How much longer can she deal with the pain

Coyotes howl into the night
Praying for mama to make things right
Have patience and you will see
Over time man will poison himself
And kill all of his own seeds
Because of his need for power and greed
He forgot what was important
He forgot how to see
That we are all part of the same tree

RECOLLECTIONS

Vision blurred cigarette burns and resin stains
Am I damned to this life or can I rise above the pain
The more I give to you the more I die
Am I strong enough to hold on to this life
As I sit here and swallow down the pain
I wonder why I let these things drive me insane
Why can't I just learn to let go
Why do these things eat at my soul
So many jumbled thoughts within my mind
Of past desires that I can't leave behind
It's like a person watching a movie
And it keeps hitting rewind
Or like a kid sitting on a bridge
Watching his life go by
So as I sit here and write upon this page
I start to think what exactly have I done today
To better myself to expand my mind
To learn how to focus on the now
And leave my past behind
To remember that because of the things I have done
I have no one but myself to blame
for what I've become

DRIFTER

The string is broken, time passes on, meet again we may
But will it be with the same sentiments and feelings
Could things ever be the same
Remembrance is a paradise that can't be driven away
And pleasure is a flower that always seems to fade
So I've been running all my life looking for truth
to make things right
Traveling and wandering the countryside
Looking for others to share the ride
What I've found so far
is there can be no rainbows without rain
And people only see what they are prepared to see
No matter how hard you want to show them the way
I've found that everything comes
if only man can find the patience to wait
Life is like an open book
but no one ever reads it the same
And every one you thought you knew
always seems to change
So I float around like a feather floating in the wind
I don't know where I'm going, just where I've been
So I take a deep breath and let the day begin
Because I know in my heart
That my path for truth starts
When I can find compassion for my fellow man

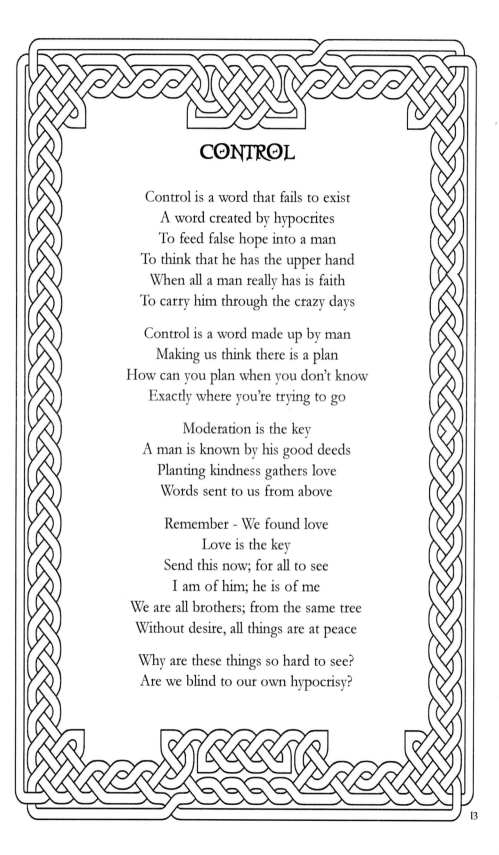

CONTROL

Control is a word that fails to exist
A word created by hypocrites
To feed false hope into a man
To think that he has the upper hand
When all a man really has is faith
To carry him through the crazy days

Control is a word made up by man
Making us think there is a plan
How can you plan when you don't know
Exactly where you're trying to go

Moderation is the key
A man is known by his good deeds
Planting kindness gathers love
Words sent to us from above

Remember - We found love
Love is the key
Send this now; for all to see
I am of him; he is of me
We are all brothers; from the same tree
Without desire, all things are at peace

Why are these things so hard to see?
Are we blind to our own hypocrisy?

LOVE

As the sand runs through my fingers like time
Pictures of moments go through my mind
Of all the people I've left behind

It's funny how things seem to change
Nothing ever stays the same
Seasons seem to come and go
And the pieces of the puzzle slowly unfold

I've learned that all together we're just a whole
Of something beautiful spinning out of control
If we could only learn to forgive and let go
Maybe we can learn to free our own souls

So love your brother he's just like you
It's just the different perspective you can't see through
So pull the veil from your eyes
And see that your own hate will plant your demise
Only through love will you find a way
To free yourself from all the pain

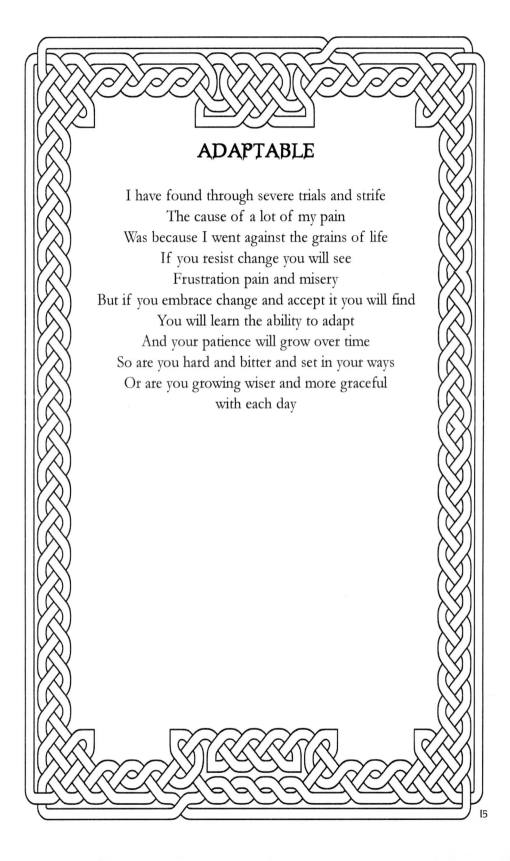

ADAPTABLE

I have found through severe trials and strife
The cause of a lot of my pain
Was because I went against the grains of life
If you resist change you will see
Frustration pain and misery
But if you embrace change and accept it you will find
You will learn the ability to adapt
And your patience will grow over time
So are you hard and bitter and set in your ways
Or are you growing wiser and more graceful
with each day

MEMORIES

What would you say to the love in your past?
Would you tell them how much you missed them?
And how much you want them back?

Memories are funny
They're sweet like a rose
They wither away
And you let them go

But the smell of her hair
Her wet lips against my face
To the curves of her skin
And her warm embrace
Entranced in a moment
That I can't let go
These moments I miss
They tear at my soul

So what would you say to the love in your past?
Would you tell them how much you missed them?
And how much you want them back?

DESIRE

Desire, she has blonde hair and blue eyes
With creamy skin and succulent thighs
Lips as tender as a new born rose
Eyes that could cut through the hardest of souls

Cleverness got her this far
Her trickiness gets her in
Her words whisper to you in the wind
Contemplations from within

Her stories tell of a secret place
Where fairies dwell and pixies lay
Where leprechauns still run and play
Unicorns still have their way

She must be a dream because now she's gone
My precious fairy has flown on
I may be a number on a belt
And put up upon a shelf

But I remember those precious days
When your touch alone made it all okay
To wake up every morning watching your face
Holding you in my warm embrace

SHOUT OUT

These beautiful women that bewilder me inside
With their rosy red lips
And their milky like thighs
Ass so round
She should win a prize
Her lotus flower so juicy
When it blooms it flows
When God made that ass
He most definitely broke the mold
To all you pimps
And all you players
Yes, even to all you ho's
Remember Cory loves you
And that's from the depths of my soul

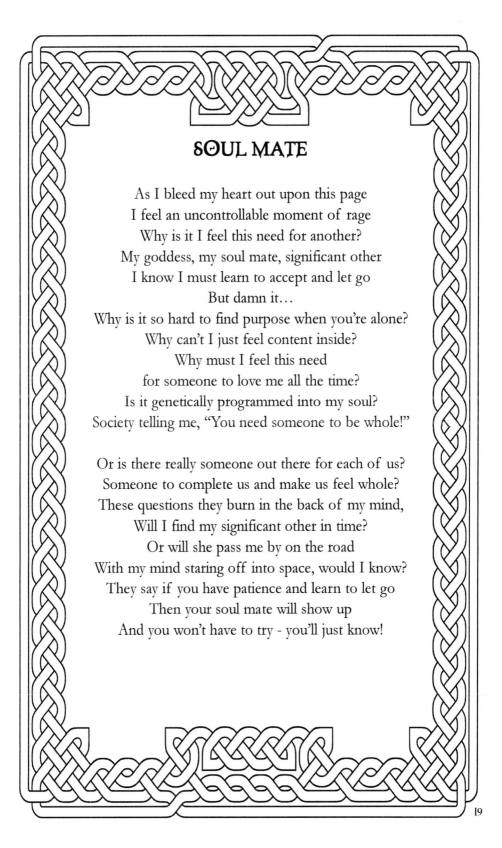

SOUL MATE

As I bleed my heart out upon this page
I feel an uncontrollable moment of rage
Why is it I feel this need for another?
My goddess, my soul mate, significant other
I know I must learn to accept and let go
But damn it…
Why is it so hard to find purpose when you're alone?
Why can't I just feel content inside?
Why must I feel this need
for someone to love me all the time?
Is it genetically programmed into my soul?
Society telling me, "You need someone to be whole!"

Or is there really someone out there for each of us?
Someone to complete us and make us feel whole?
These questions they burn in the back of my mind,
Will I find my significant other in time?
Or will she pass me by on the road
With my mind staring off into space, would I know?
They say if you have patience and learn to let go
Then your soul mate will show up
And you won't have to try - you'll just know!

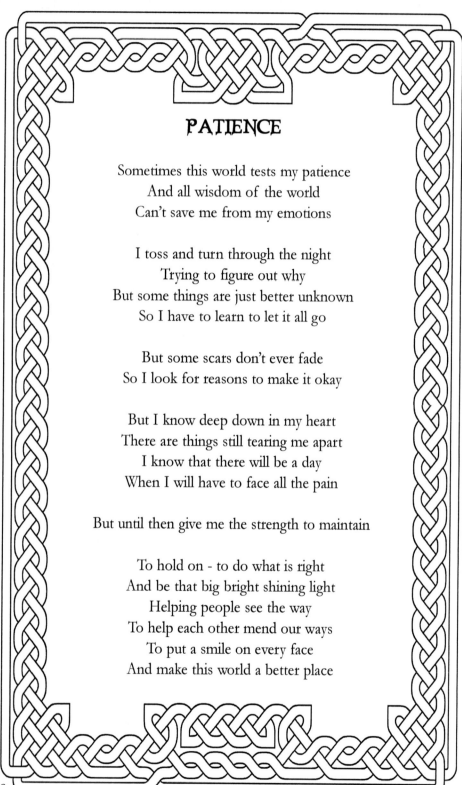

PATIENCE

Sometimes this world tests my patience
And all wisdom of the world
Can't save me from my emotions

I toss and turn through the night
Trying to figure out why
But some things are just better unknown
So I have to learn to let it all go

But some scars don't ever fade
So I look for reasons to make it okay

But I know deep down in my heart
There are things still tearing me apart
I know that there will be a day
When I will have to face all the pain

But until then give me the strength to maintain

To hold on - to do what is right
And be that big bright shining light
Helping people see the way
To help each other mend our ways
To put a smile on every face
And make this world a better place

SECOND CHANCE

Is she an angel
Or is she the devil's advocate in disguise
Is she telling me truth or feeding me lies
So I sit here patiently waiting to find
The answers to these questions
that burn within my mind
Does she really love me
Can we make it work this time
Is it worth it to me to put my heart on the line
Because this may be my last if she cuts me this time
But first I must learn to let go
Of this past between us that tears at my soul
So God here I go one last time
Planting love in hopes that I'll find
This beautiful garden within my mind
Where two lovers co-exist
and I find there is something more
Than just a few moments of bliss
That there truly is something more to this
That there is purpose in all this madness
So here I go clenching my fist
Hoping I find love in all of this

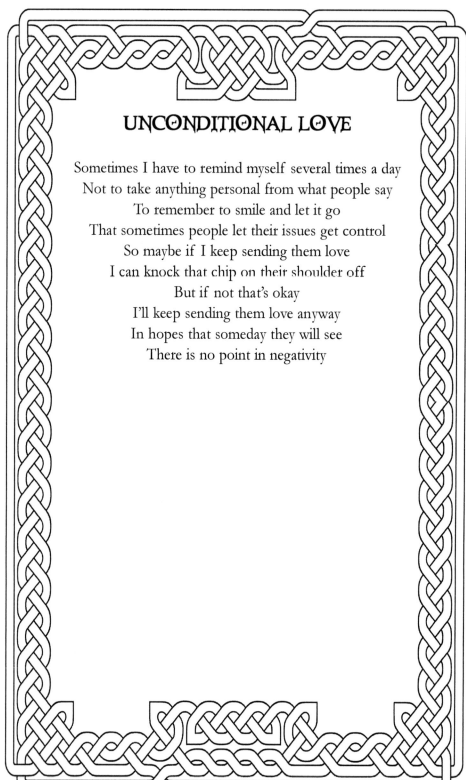

UNCONDITIONAL LOVE

Sometimes I have to remind myself several times a day
Not to take anything personal from what people say
To remember to smile and let it go
That sometimes people let their issues get control
So maybe if I keep sending them love
I can knock that chip on their shoulder off
But if not that's okay
I'll keep sending them love anyway
In hopes that someday they will see
There is no point in negativity

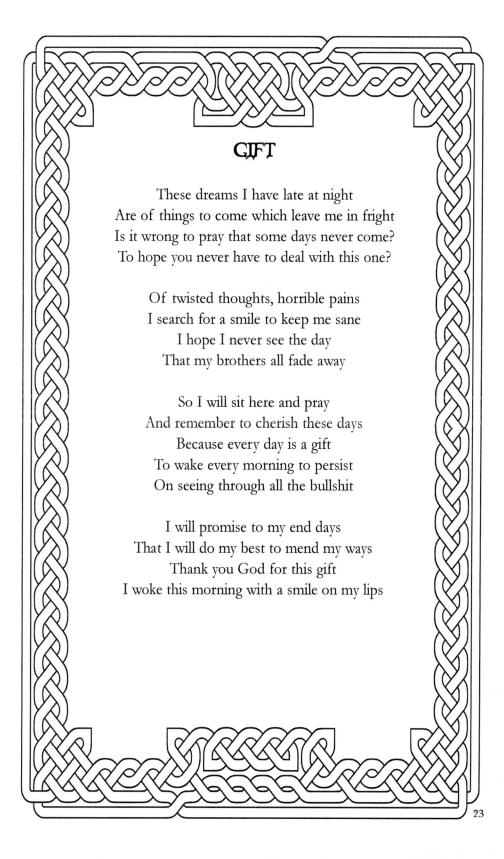

GIFT

These dreams I have late at night
Are of things to come which leave me in fright
Is it wrong to pray that some days never come?
To hope you never have to deal with this one?

Of twisted thoughts, horrible pains
I search for a smile to keep me sane
I hope I never see the day
That my brothers all fade away

So I will sit here and pray
And remember to cherish these days
Because every day is a gift
To wake every morning to persist
On seeing through all the bullshit

I will promise to my end days
That I will do my best to mend my ways
Thank you God for this gift
I woke this morning with a smile on my lips

CHANGE

How many times have you walked this road?
Where lovers rip out your heart
And stomp on your soul
All these pictures go through my mind
Of all the people that I've left behind
I try so hard to mend these regrets
But the scars are so deep I can never forget
So I get up each day trying to let go
In hopes that I don't become bitter and old
But like I said some things don't ever fade
But still I have hope that I'll find a way
To mend my heart, to repair my soul
To know when it's time
To let it all go
To realize this every day:
All things in life must eventually change

SECOND PATH: MENTAL

CLARITY

The situation fails to matter
It's what you do with it, you see?
You cannot control the moment
But you can control how you perceive
Acceptance, denial, and conviction
Prevent understanding of a situation
So let your mind and the speakers mind move free
And through your awareness and sensitivity
You will see
The possibility
Of a true community

So don't start from a conclusion
Above all
There must be a state of choiceless awareness
Without a sense of comparison at all
This will enable you to see
The world in a moment of clarity

BIG PICTURE

Sometimes memories come up in the back of my mind
I wonder if they were a figment of my imagination the whole
time
Then I wonder about the paradox in time
How past and future are only in my mind
And if this is so then the only truth is now
So future and past are expectations and perspectives
made up by man
Trying to explain a moment that no longer exists at hand
The breath is a beautiful thing that shows so much
You breathe in embrace and hold
Then you breathe out and let go
This is how we should be
But somehow we get caught up in our personal needs
And forgot how to see
The bigger picture of things beyond you and me

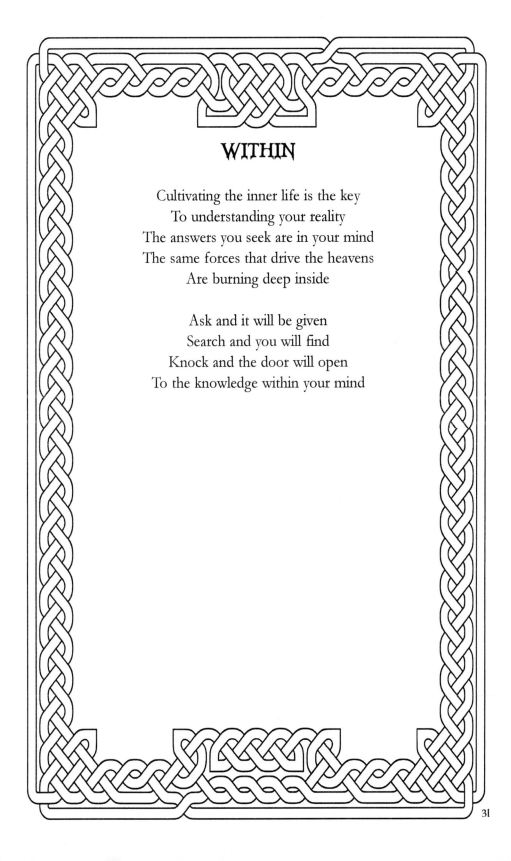

WITHIN

Cultivating the inner life is the key
To understanding your reality
The answers you seek are in your mind
The same forces that drive the heavens
Are burning deep inside

Ask and it will be given
Search and you will find
Knock and the door will open
To the knowledge within your mind

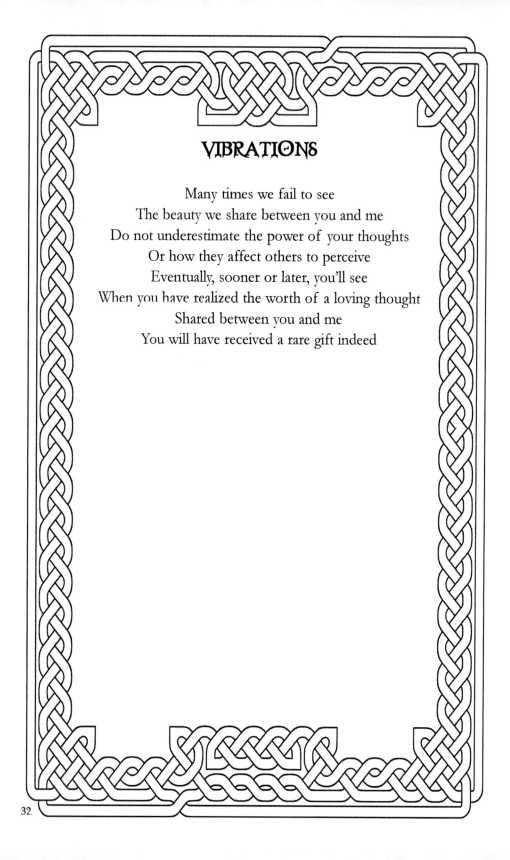

VIBRATIONS

Many times we fail to see
The beauty we share between you and me
Do not underestimate the power of your thoughts
Or how they affect others to perceive
Eventually, sooner or later, you'll see
When you have realized the worth of a loving thought
Shared between you and me
You will have received a rare gift indeed

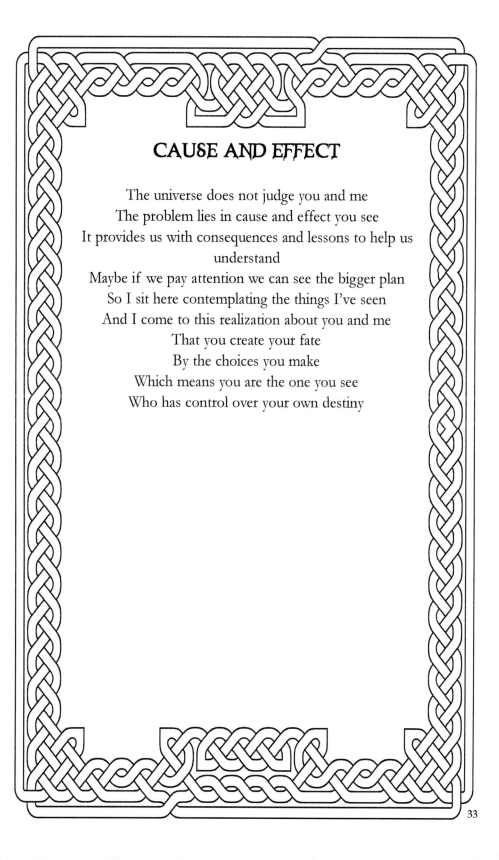

CAUSE AND EFFECT

The universe does not judge you and me
The problem lies in cause and effect you see
It provides us with consequences and lessons to help us
understand
Maybe if we pay attention we can see the bigger plan
So I sit here contemplating the things I've seen
And I come to this realization about you and me
That you create your fate
By the choices you make
Which means you are the one you see
Who has control over your own destiny

DS '06

FLOW

A good fighter must sense rather than perceive
Just let nature take its course
Be patient you'll see

Flow like the water
Bend like a reed
The mind must be quiet and calm like the sea

Simply feel the opponent's moves
Like that of a stream that forever flows
And adjust ones self accordingly
Shifting from moment to moment
This is what we call flow

CONTEMPLATIONS

If you could see the world through my eyes
The beauty you would see
would bring tears to your eyes
You finally come to the realization
There is no difference between you and I

As I run my fingers through the dirt
I sit and contemplate the earth
How seasons seem to come and go
And how the spiral's spinning out of control

Could this be the end days?
Will man learn to mend his ways?
Or is this the way it's supposed to be?
Are we the ones who control our own destiny?

As these questions go through my mind
I wander aimlessly through the countryside
Looking for others who might know
The answers to this puzzle I hold

Wisdom has taught me
To be patient and kind
And that the answers I seek
Will come in time

But first I must learn to control
These emotions and thoughts spinning out of control

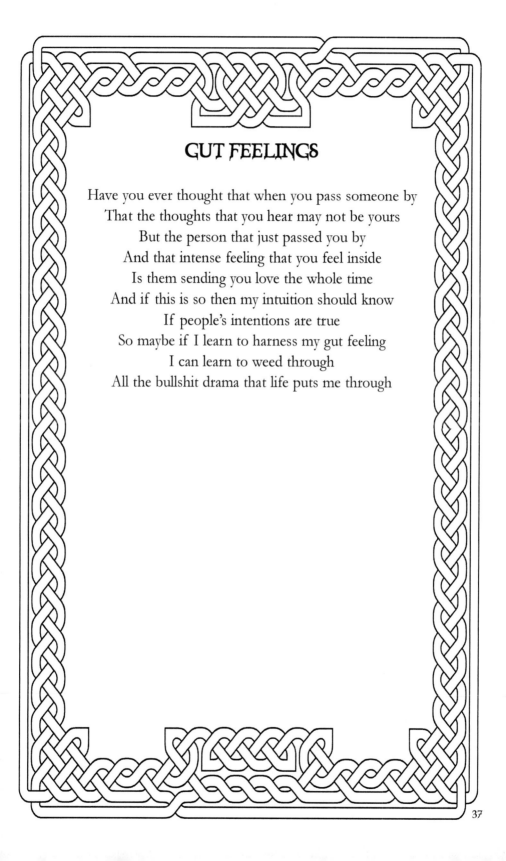

GUT FEELINGS

Have you ever thought that when you pass someone by
That the thoughts that you hear may not be yours
But the person that just passed you by
And that intense feeling that you feel inside
Is them sending you love the whole time
And if this is so then my intuition should know
If people's intentions are true
So maybe if I learn to harness my gut feeling
I can learn to weed through
All the bullshit drama that life puts me through

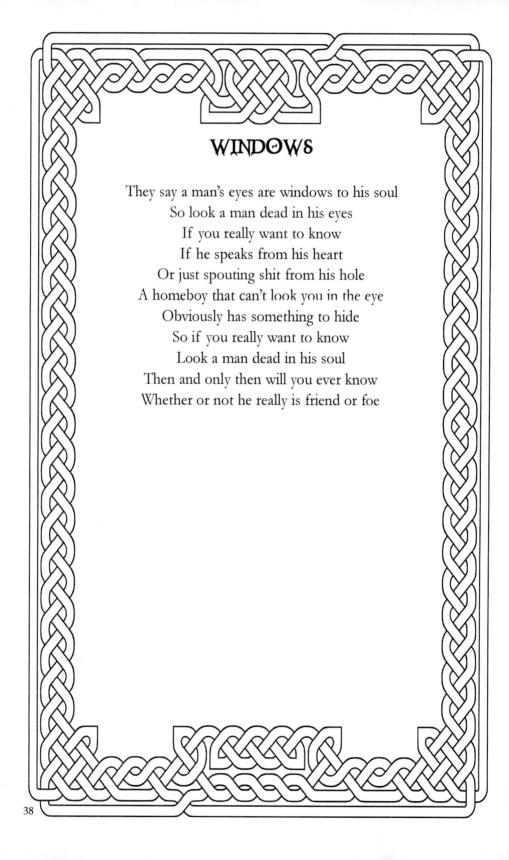

WINDOWS

They say a man's eyes are windows to his soul
So look a man dead in his eyes
If you really want to know
If he speaks from his heart
Or just spouting shit from his hole
A homeboy that can't look you in the eye
Obviously has something to hide
So if you really want to know
Look a man dead in his soul
Then and only then will you ever know
Whether or not he really is friend or foe

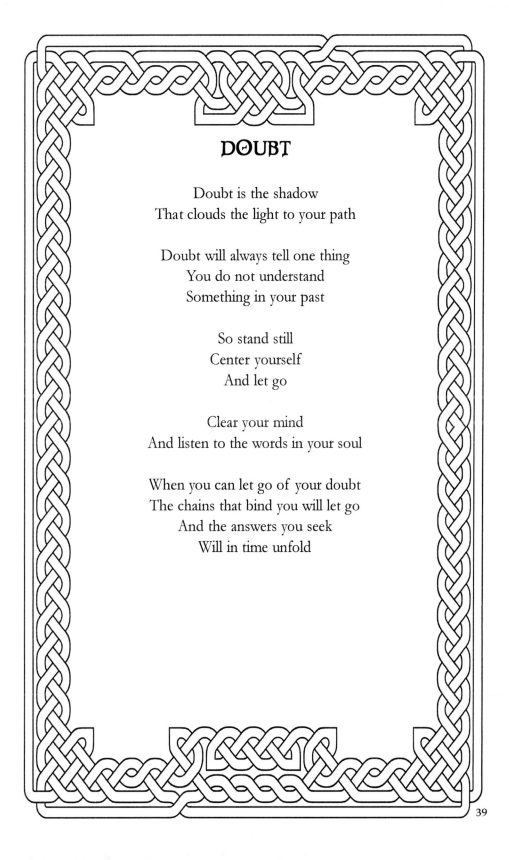

DOUBT

Doubt is the shadow
That clouds the light to your path

Doubt will always tell one thing
You do not understand
Something in your past

So stand still
Center yourself
And let go

Clear your mind
And listen to the words in your soul

When you can let go of your doubt
The chains that bind you will let go
And the answers you seek
Will in time unfold

EMPATHY

As I sit and look at my friends I see
All the different perspectives of what I could be
Then I think of the choices I've made
And all the things that I've seen
What does all of this mean to me
I see that each of us has a piece of the puzzle to unfold
That maybe if I pay close attention
I can figure out which part of the puzzle that I hold
That as the veil grows thin I begin to see
Each person that I meet has a lesson for me
That if I look close enough I can see
All the beautiful synchronicity
How our lives inner twine
With each choice that we make
That every day I open my eyes
Time flies a little faster each day
As my compassion grows for my fellow man
I learn empathy is one of the hardest lessons
to comprehend

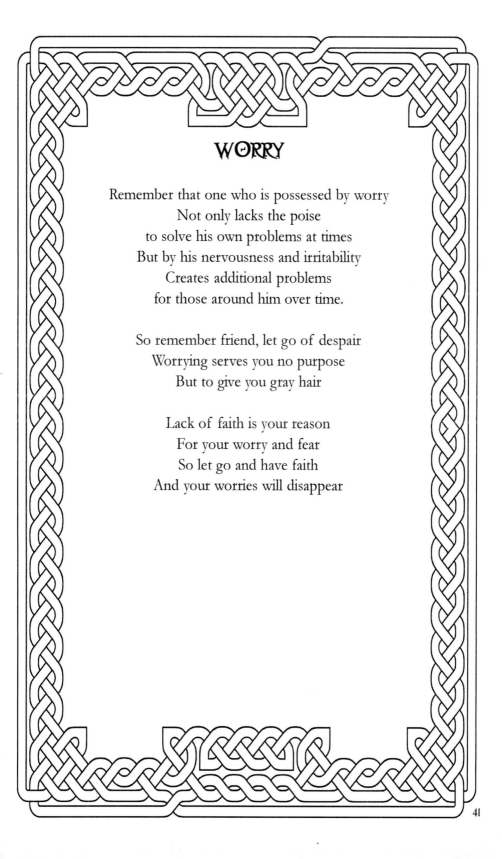

WORRY

Remember that one who is possessed by worry
Not only lacks the poise
to solve his own problems at times
But by his nervousness and irritability
Creates additional problems
for those around him over time.

So remember friend, let go of despair
Worrying serves you no purpose
But to give you gray hair

Lack of faith is your reason
For your worry and fear
So let go and have faith
And your worries will disappear

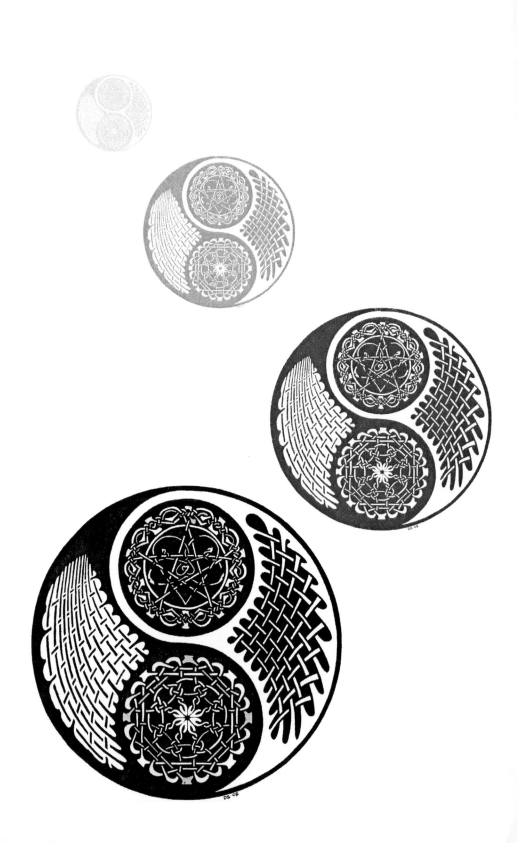

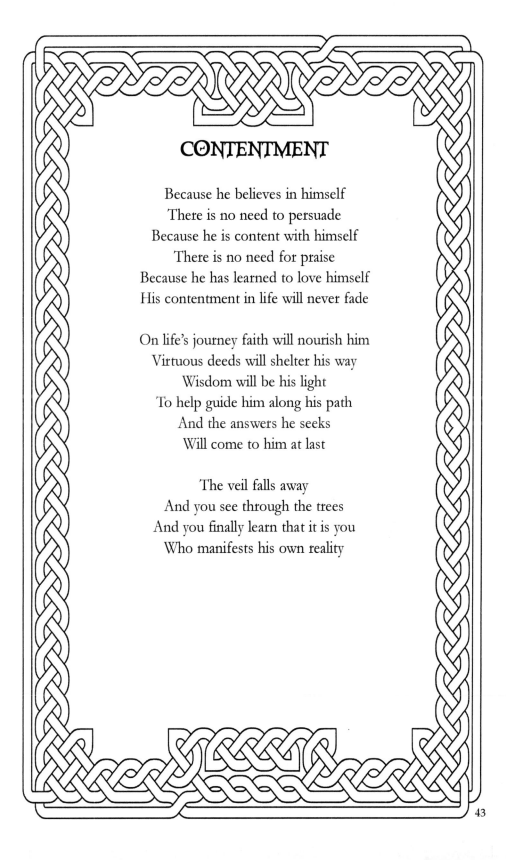

CONTENTMENT

Because he believes in himself
There is no need to persuade
Because he is content with himself
There is no need for praise
Because he has learned to love himself
His contentment in life will never fade

On life's journey faith will nourish him
Virtuous deeds will shelter his way
Wisdom will be his light
To help guide him along his path
And the answers he seeks
Will come to him at last

The veil falls away
And you see through the trees
And you finally learn that it is you
Who manifests his own reality

DS '06

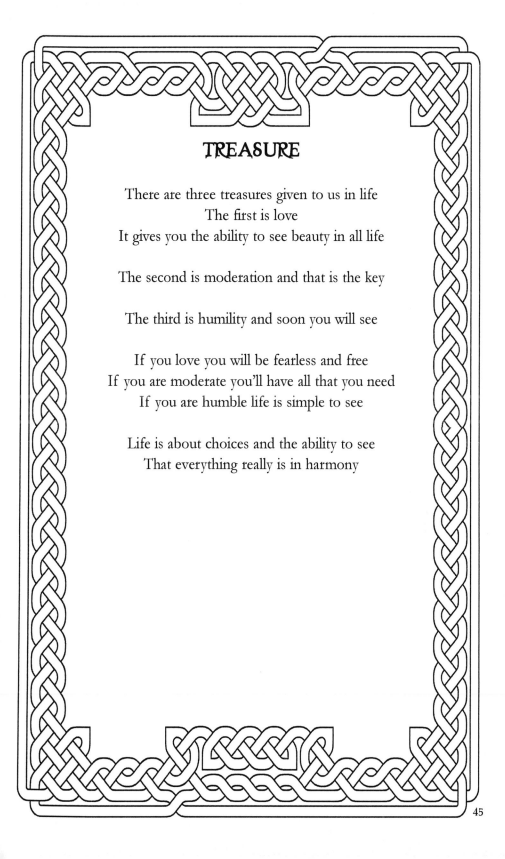

TREASURE

There are three treasures given to us in life
The first is love
It gives you the ability to see beauty in all life

The second is moderation and that is the key

The third is humility and soon you will see

If you love you will be fearless and free
If you are moderate you'll have all that you need
If you are humble life is simple to see

Life is about choices and the ability to see
That everything really is in harmony

PENDULUM

As a child I grew up to believe
That to be strong was having the ability to hold on

As I grow older I come to find
That it is the ability to know when to let go
That makes me strong inside

So over the years I have come to believe
That I must learn to balance the pendulum
that is inside of me

MODERATION

We know beauty because there is ugly
We know there is good because there is bad
We know being ends in not being
And to be without something
You must first have

Long defines short
High equals low
You can't have one without the other
Or there would be no such thing as a whole

The wise teach without telling
And allow without commands
To have without possessing
To love without demands

Moderation is the key
To a happy soul
You must first learn how to balance
Before you can learn to be whole

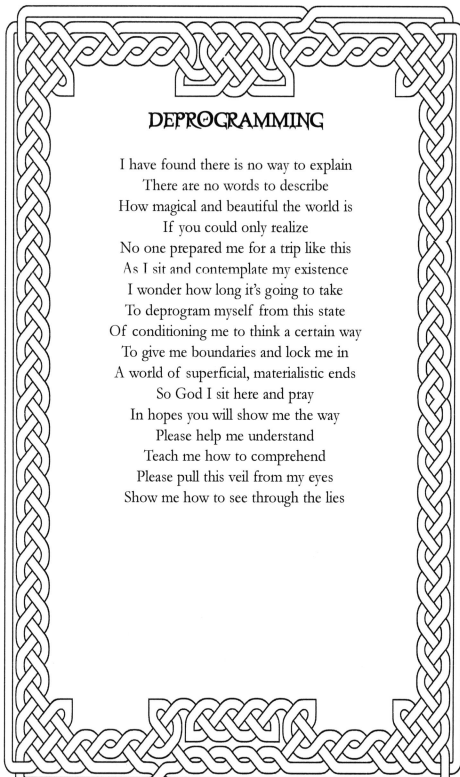

DEPROGRAMMING

I have found there is no way to explain
There are no words to describe
How magical and beautiful the world is
If you could only realize
No one prepared me for a trip like this
As I sit and contemplate my existence
I wonder how long it's going to take
To deprogram myself from this state
Of conditioning me to think a certain way
To give me boundaries and lock me in
A world of superficial, materialistic ends
So God I sit here and pray
In hopes you will show me the way
Please help me understand
Teach me how to comprehend
Please pull this veil from my eyes
Show me how to see through the lies

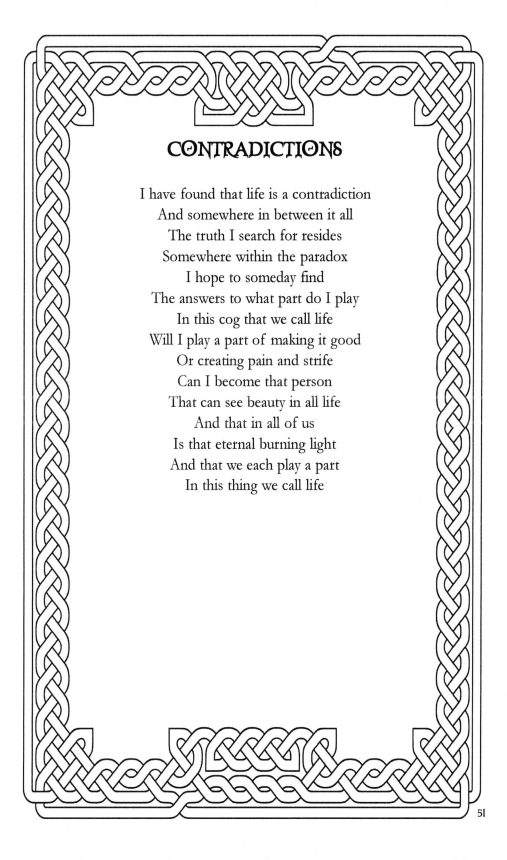

CONTRADICTIONS

I have found that life is a contradiction
And somewhere in between it all
The truth I search for resides
Somewhere within the paradox
I hope to someday find
The answers to what part do I play
In this cog that we call life
Will I play a part of making it good
Or creating pain and strife
Can I become that person
That can see beauty in all life
And that in all of us
Is that eternal burning light
And that we each play a part
In this thing we call life

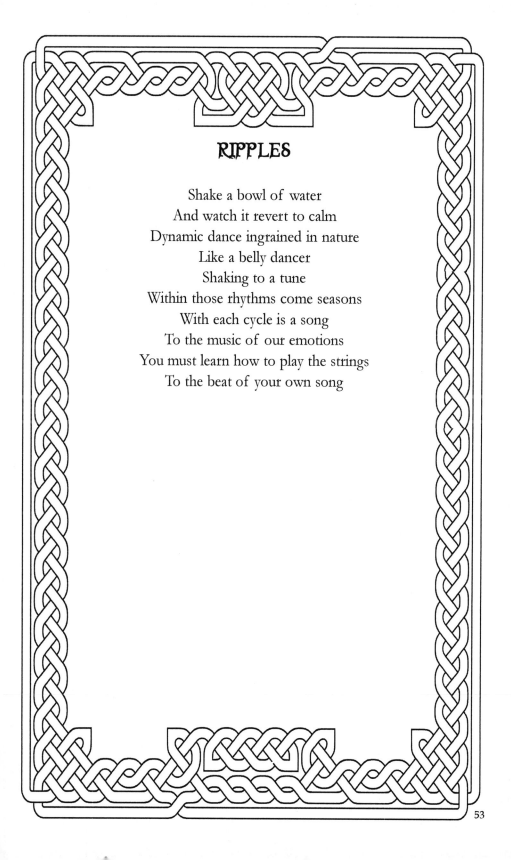

RIPPLES

Shake a bowl of water
And watch it revert to calm
Dynamic dance ingrained in nature
Like a belly dancer
Shaking to a tune
Within those rhythms come seasons
With each cycle is a song
To the music of our emotions
You must learn how to play the strings
To the beat of your own song

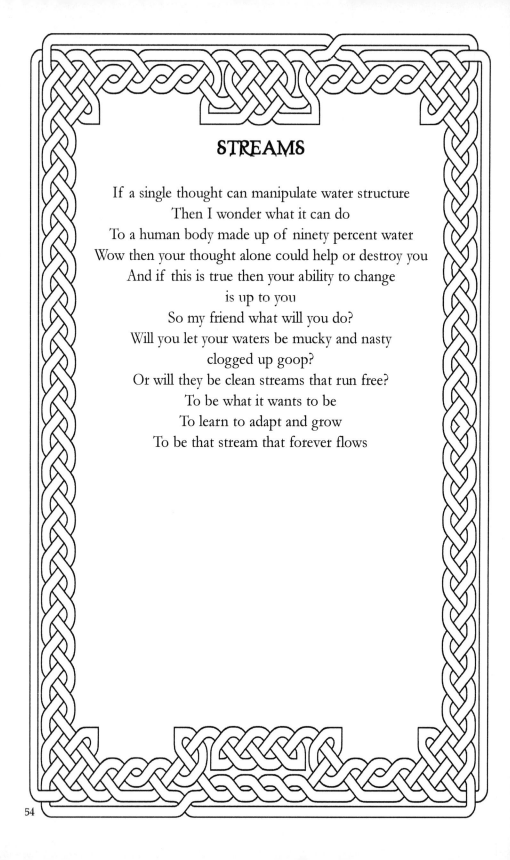

STREAMS

If a single thought can manipulate water structure
Then I wonder what it can do
To a human body made up of ninety percent water
Wow then your thought alone could help or destroy you
And if this is true then your ability to change
is up to you
So my friend what will you do?
Will you let your waters be mucky and nasty
clogged up goop?
Or will they be clean streams that run free?
To be what it wants to be
To learn to adapt and grow
To be that stream that forever flows

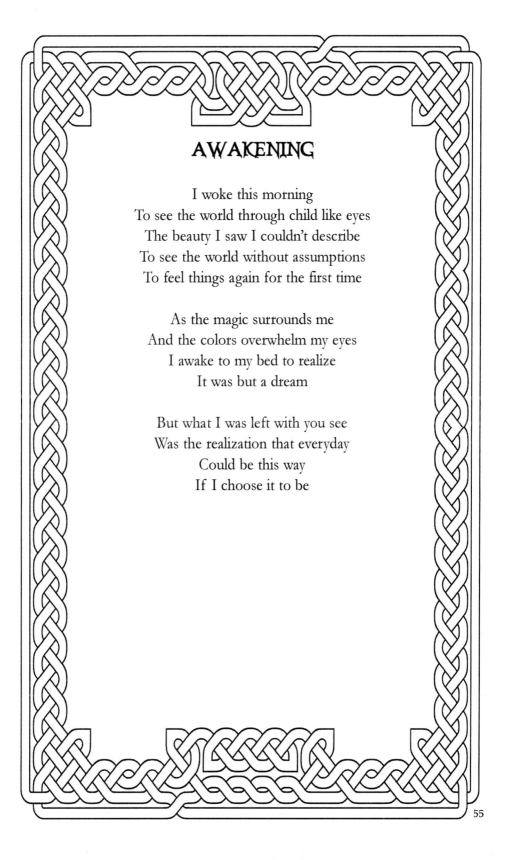

AWAKENING

I woke this morning
To see the world through child like eyes
The beauty I saw I couldn't describe
To see the world without assumptions
To feel things again for the first time

As the magic surrounds me
And the colors overwhelm my eyes
I awake to my bed to realize
It was but a dream

But what I was left with you see
Was the realization that everyday
Could be this way
If I choose it to be

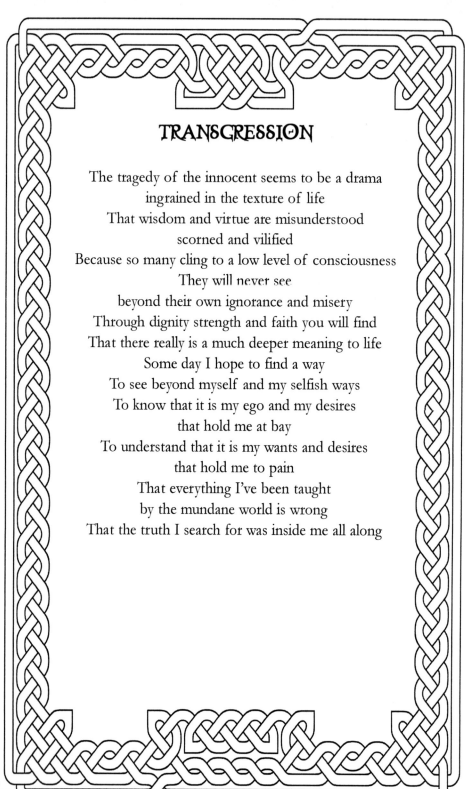

TRANSGRESSION

The tragedy of the innocent seems to be a drama
ingrained in the texture of life
That wisdom and virtue are misunderstood
scorned and vilified
Because so many cling to a low level of consciousness
They will never see
beyond their own ignorance and misery
Through dignity strength and faith you will find
That there really is a much deeper meaning to life
Some day I hope to find a way
To see beyond myself and my selfish ways
To know that it is my ego and my desires
that hold me at bay
To understand that it is my wants and desires
that hold me to pain
That everything I've been taught
by the mundane world is wrong
That the truth I search for was inside me all along

INNER SANCTUM

So as I sit here and reminisce
I think about all the stupid shit
I question why I can't shake this pain
So please someone help me comprehend before I go insane
Cause I feel like I'm on this endless race
Lord please give me strength to keep up this pace
Because I see the world as a reflection
Each person is a different perspective of you and me
So when I get irritated and I feel the world is against me
I realize it's just a part inside of me that I don't like to see
Universe how much longer
before I learn to let go of this ego
And stop wasting time
And stop blaming others
when I know that the drama is only in my mind
To know that the cause of my irritation
Comes from my expectations
Or assumptions that were never meant to be
I realize that the problem stems from
The way I was taught to perceive
That I need to let go of these delusions
Of the way things are supposed to be
And learn to forgive myself and others
So I can be open to receive
And experience life to the fullest degree

THIRD PATH: SPIRITUAL

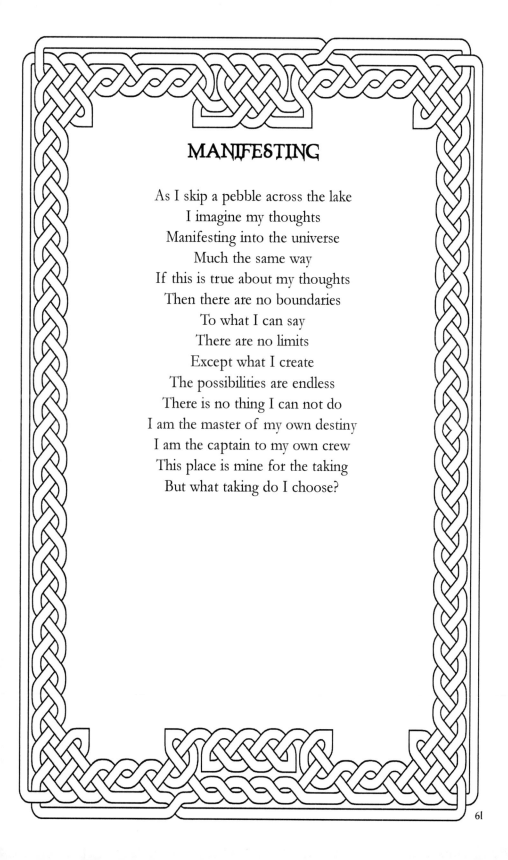

MANIFESTING

As I skip a pebble across the lake
I imagine my thoughts
Manifesting into the universe
Much the same way
If this is true about my thoughts
Then there are no boundaries
To what I can say
There are no limits
Except what I create
The possibilities are endless
There is no thing I can not do
I am the master of my own destiny
I am the captain to my own crew
This place is mine for the taking
But what taking do I choose?

PIECES

Life is something for which there is no answer
It must be understood from moment to moment,
you'll see
The answer you find inevitably
Comes from the pattern you wish to perceive
So if you don't mind me asking
What do you actually see?
Maybe if we work together
We will find the pieces we need
I am told that pain is just weakness leaving the body
And that it's good for the soul
That a man with a slow tongue
And a quick eye
Can walk away untarnished and whole
Unity is formless
And formless is the whole
Only by choice will we ever know
That it is our free will to choose
That separates us from the whole

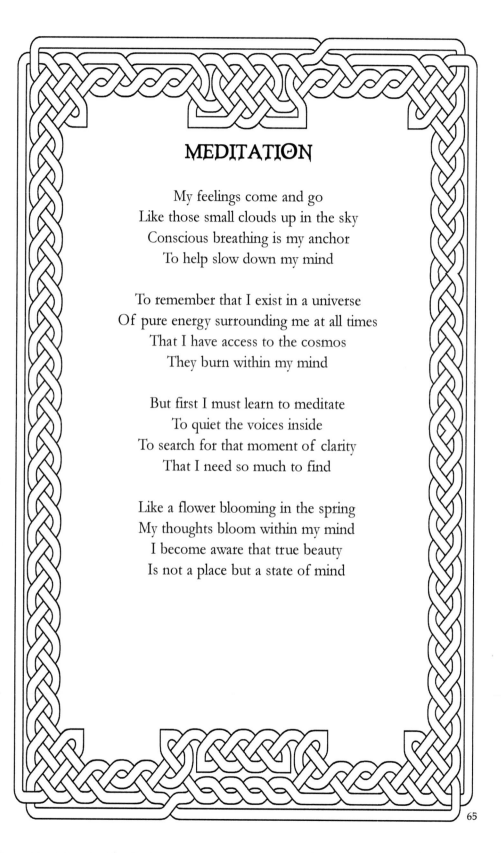

MEDITATION

My feelings come and go
Like those small clouds up in the sky
Conscious breathing is my anchor
To help slow down my mind

To remember that I exist in a universe
Of pure energy surrounding me at all times
That I have access to the cosmos
They burn within my mind

But first I must learn to meditate
To quiet the voices inside
To search for that moment of clarity
That I need so much to find

Like a flower blooming in the spring
My thoughts bloom within my mind
I become aware that true beauty
Is not a place but a state of mind

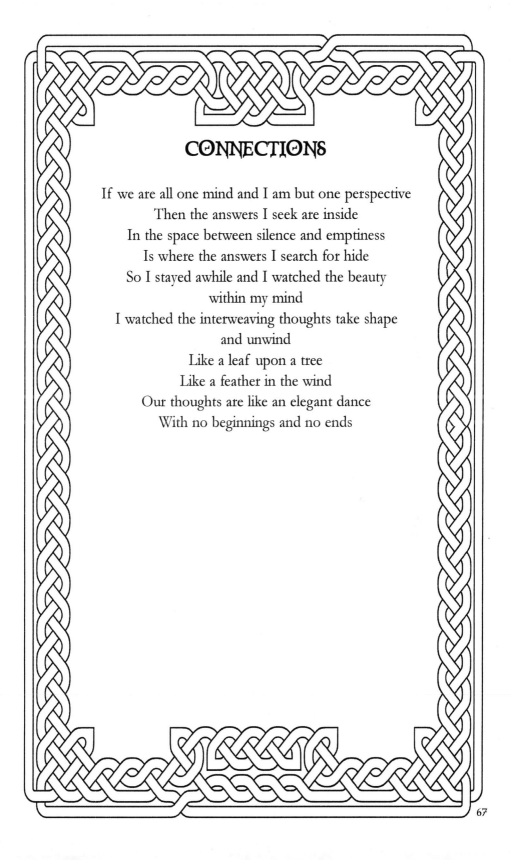

CONNECTIONS

If we are all one mind and I am but one perspective
Then the answers I seek are inside
In the space between silence and emptiness
Is where the answers I search for hide
So I stayed awhile and I watched the beauty
within my mind
I watched the interweaving thoughts take shape
and unwind
Like a leaf upon a tree
Like a feather in the wind
Our thoughts are like an elegant dance
With no beginnings and no ends

JOURNEY

Contemplations from within
Is where it all has to begin
To ponder the question of who you are
To where are you going?
And exactly how far?

Why are you here?
Do you really know?
Do these contemplations tear at your soul?
From the back of the mind
The answers unfold

Be patient my son
Time moves at its own speed
Don't be in such a rush
The answers will come
I promise you'll see

The destination will be what it will be
Be mindful of each moment and soon you will see
The journey is in each moment that you breathe

(I wrote this poem in the middle of the night, January 12, 2005, to wake up to find my Grandmother Betty died in her sleep from a heart attack. Thank you Grandmother for the words of wisdom. I won't forget.)

MISFORTUNES

A great man does not think before hand
Of his words that they may be sincere and true
He is patient and kind
Not arrogant or rude

A mind immune to emotional influences
Like a river in constant flow
He uses the stones life throws at him
For the path along the road

It is through our misfortunes
That we learn to adapt and grow
It is when you feel most like giving up
That you are closest to your goal

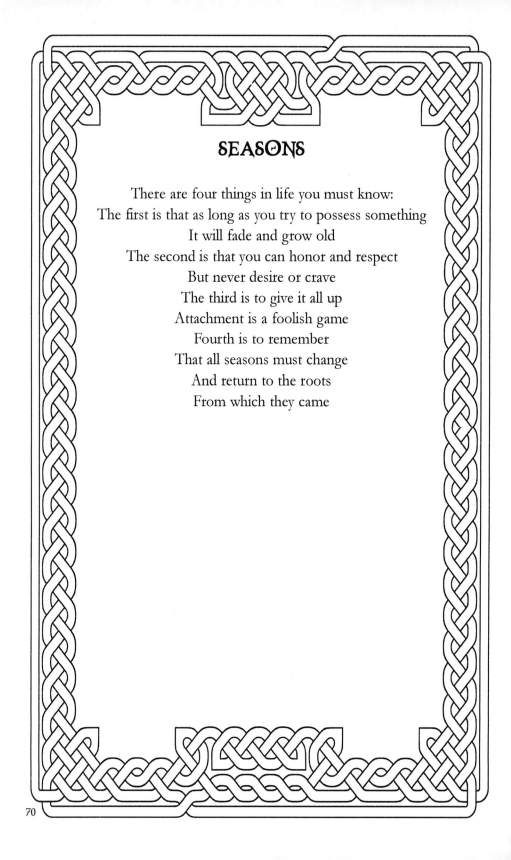

SEASONS

There are four things in life you must know:
The first is that as long as you try to possess something
It will fade and grow old
The second is that you can honor and respect
But never desire or crave
The third is to give it all up
Attachment is a foolish game
Fourth is to remember
That all seasons must change
And return to the roots
From which they came

PERSPECTIVES

Once when I was a child I had a dream
That I saw this guy in a puddle smiling back at me
He had long hair and rugged beard
With these piercing blue eyes
So I sat and pondered many of my days
Wondering who the hell is this guy?
But as I got older I began to see
That the guy in that puddle was just me
Smiling back at me
Then I thought to myself
is this the path that is destined for me
Or am I just wandering aimlessly
So is it my intuition that guides the way
Or is it me who creates my own purpose along the way
But the wisdom I seek comes with time so they say
To cultivate patience
To listen to what my brothers and sisters have to say
Maybe if we learn to listen
We can find a better way
To push the boundaries to see at last
That I hold the key to these shackles that hold me back
That it is up to me to be the student
Who can find the teacher inside
To see that every moment is a lesson
if you look at it right

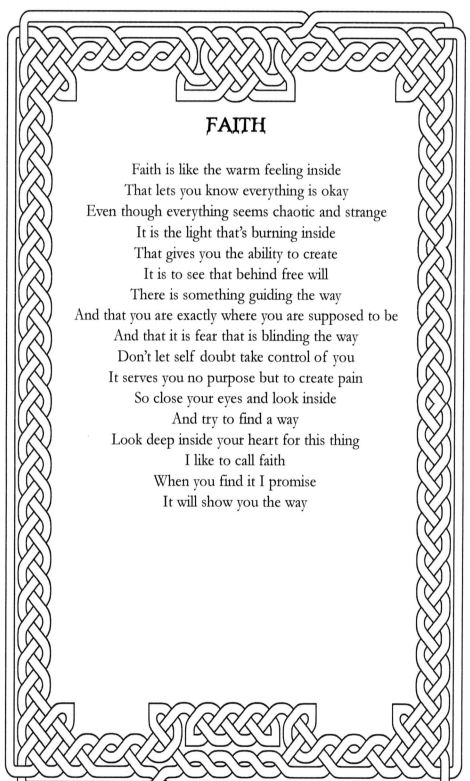

FAITH

Faith is like the warm feeling inside
That lets you know everything is okay
Even though everything seems chaotic and strange
It is the light that's burning inside
That gives you the ability to create
It is to see that behind free will
There is something guiding the way
And that you are exactly where you are supposed to be
And that it is fear that is blinding the way
Don't let self doubt take control of you
It serves you no purpose but to create pain
So close your eyes and look inside
And try to find a way
Look deep inside your heart for this thing
I like to call faith
When you find it I promise
It will show you the way

EMOTIONS

I try to imagine the world as an ocean
And our emotions are like waves crashing into the sea
And if you look at the world in this manner
you begin to see
That with every moment of joy and happiness
Pain and sorrow will surely be
That with every moment of laughter and bliss
There is tears and misery
That every time you say hello
there's sure to be a goodbye
So as my life passes before me like a blink of an eye
I look at the waves crash and I begin to realize
That with every goodbye there is sure to be a hello
That with every tear shed joy is sure to follow
So I wake up each day and cast my sails to the wind
With hope in my eyes and faith as my friend
I hear a small voice from inside me say
Look deep in your heart and you shall find
That through your tribulations and trials
within your mind
Your empathy will grow and you will find
That I was there walking beside you
Embracing you in love the whole time

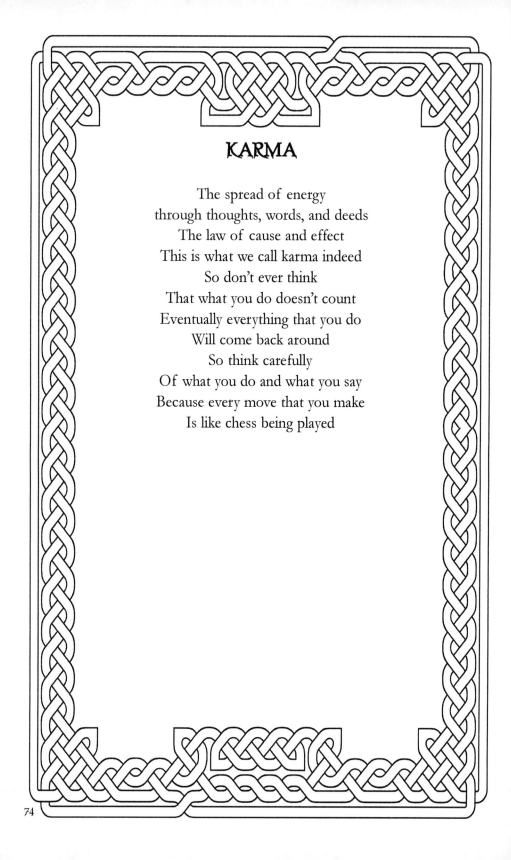

KARMA

The spread of energy
through thoughts, words, and deeds
The law of cause and effect
This is what we call karma indeed
So don't ever think
That what you do doesn't count
Eventually everything that you do
Will come back around
So think carefully
Of what you do and what you say
Because every move that you make
Is like chess being played

FRUSTRATION

Never try to drag a friend into the light
No matter how much you think you're right
It's not that people can't comprehend
It's just they have their own means to their ends
So just stand back and let the drama unfold
If they need you for help
I'm sure they'll let you know
So embrace them in love
And tell them that they're okay
To remember that we all have our days

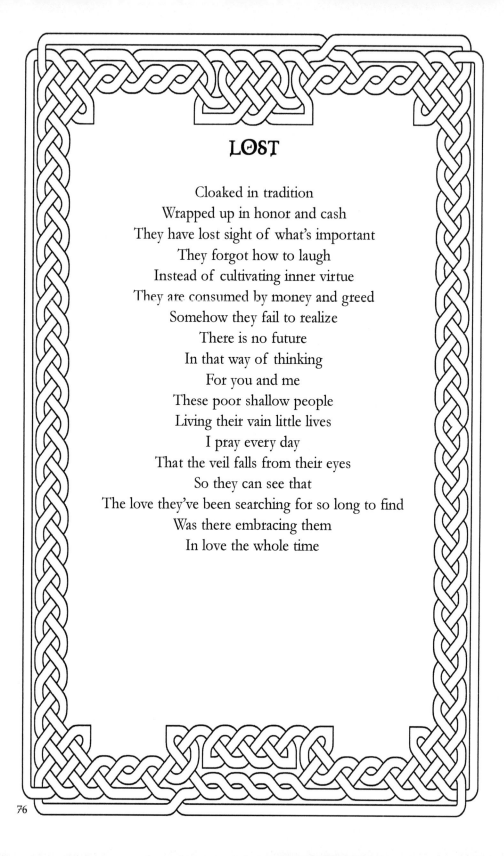

LOST

Cloaked in tradition
Wrapped up in honor and cash
They have lost sight of what's important
They forgot how to laugh
Instead of cultivating inner virtue
They are consumed by money and greed
Somehow they fail to realize
There is no future
In that way of thinking
For you and me
These poor shallow people
Living their vain little lives
I pray every day
That the veil falls from their eyes
So they can see that
The love they've been searching for so long to find
Was there embracing them
In love the whole time

UNITY

If you are my reflection and I am yours
Then I guess the question at hand
Is how can I help you my friend
What are you searching for?
Do you even know?
Which direction are you heading?
Is that where you're trying to go?
Every time I help someone
I feel this beautiful feeling inside
It's like a moment of tranquility
That I can not hide
I come to a moment of realization
That every time I help someone
That good feeling I feel inside
Is because in all reality
I am just helping myself out the whole time

DS 06

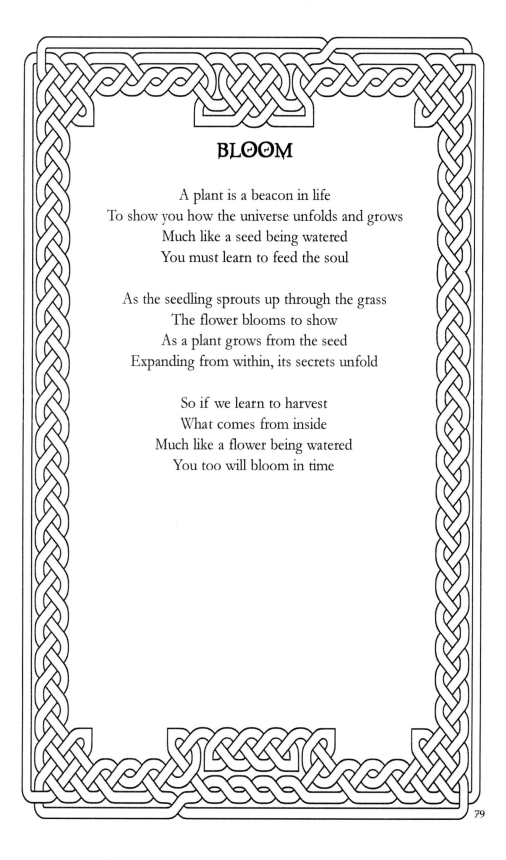

BLOOM

A plant is a beacon in life
To show you how the universe unfolds and grows
Much like a seed being watered
You must learn to feed the soul

As the seedling sprouts up through the grass
The flower blooms to show
As a plant grows from the seed
Expanding from within, its secrets unfold

So if we learn to harvest
What comes from inside
Much like a flower being watered
You too will bloom in time

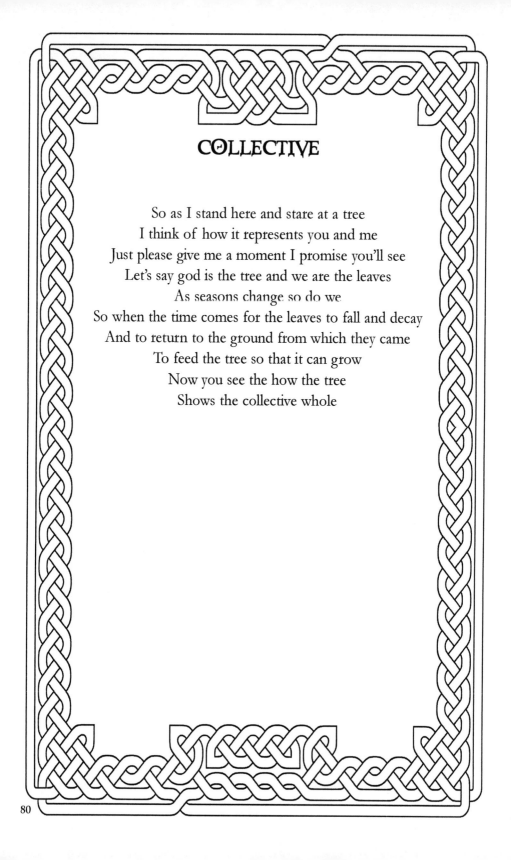

COLLECTIVE

So as I stand here and stare at a tree
I think of how it represents you and me
Just please give me a moment I promise you'll see
Let's say god is the tree and we are the leaves
As seasons change so do we
So when the time comes for the leaves to fall and decay
And to return to the ground from which they came
To feed the tree so that it can grow
Now you see the how the tree
Shows the collective whole

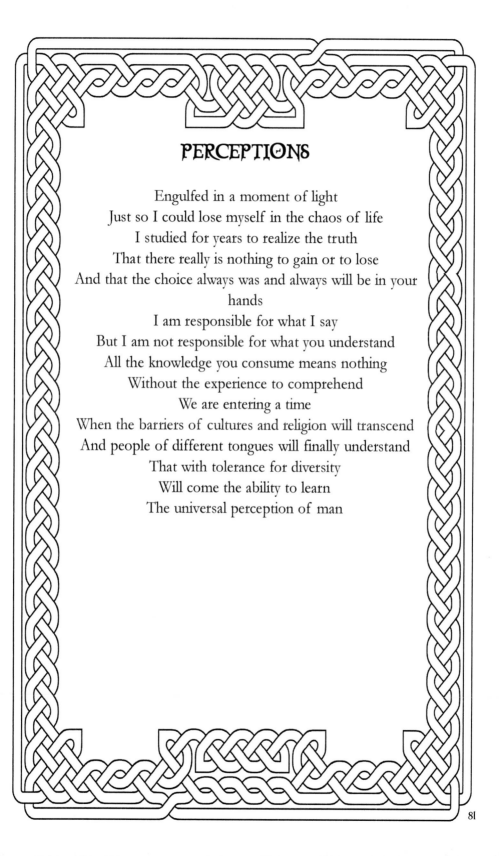

PERCEPTIONS

Engulfed in a moment of light
Just so I could lose myself in the chaos of life
I studied for years to realize the truth
That there really is nothing to gain or to lose
And that the choice always was and always will be in your
hands
I am responsible for what I say
But I am not responsible for what you understand
All the knowledge you consume means nothing
Without the experience to comprehend
We are entering a time
When the barriers of cultures and religion will transcend
And people of different tongues will finally understand
That with tolerance for diversity
Will come the ability to learn
The universal perception of man

INTUITION

There are no words to express
There is no way to reveal
There is no way to explain
Who's steering the wheel

This inner force that burns inside
That gives me purpose on which to thrive
As I walk this windy road
Wandering off into the unknown

These beautiful visions go through my mind
And a tiny voice speaks from inside
It tells me how blessed I am to be alive
To enjoy these moments as they go by

So I close my eyes to meditate
Suddenly I feel this warm embrace
Oh hello there my friend
Where did you go?

Are the hippies ready to go?
Let's hurry up I can't wait to climb
Those beautiful mountains
So I can unwind
So I can hear the drum beats roll
God it's good to finally be home

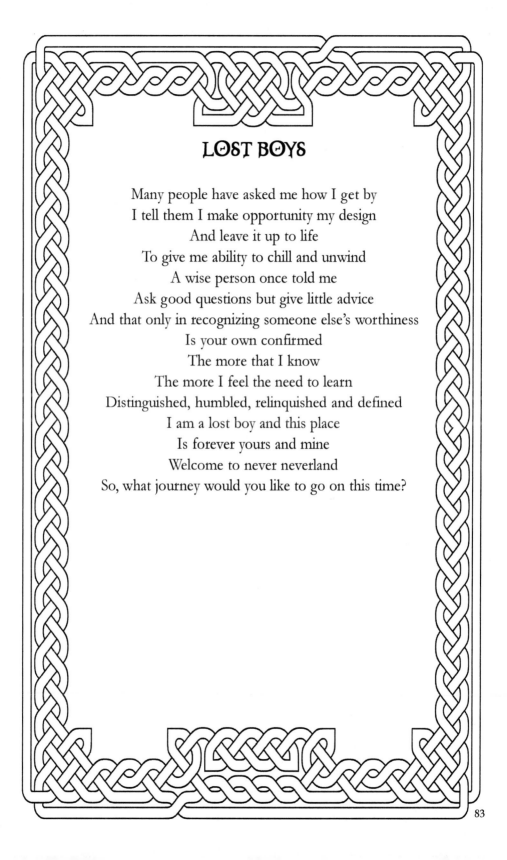

LOST BOYS

Many people have asked me how I get by
I tell them I make opportunity my design
And leave it up to life
To give me ability to chill and unwind
A wise person once told me
Ask good questions but give little advice
And that only in recognizing someone else's worthiness
Is your own confirmed
The more that I know
The more I feel the need to learn
Distinguished, humbled, relinquished and defined
I am a lost boy and this place
Is forever yours and mine
Welcome to never neverland
So, what journey would you like to go on this time?

LESSNS

As I sit here and watch my hand bleed
I wonder how much of this is real to me
How much of this is mental
How much of this is true
If everything I've been taught is bullshit
And this really is an illusion
that I'm just passing through
Like the caterpillar turning into the butterfly
Maybe it's just hard to see through the cocoon
So all these lessons that I've learned
Are like layers that I'm peeling through
Eventually through my struggles
I will learn to make anew
And through my tribulations and studies
This is what I leave to you:

The greatest help is self-help, this is no lie;
Knowing is not enough, we must learn to apply;
Willing is not enough, we must learn to do;
These, my friend, are the three lessons that I leave to you.